DREAMING OF AN ANCIENT COUNTRY
PASSAGES FROM
VIRGIL'S 'GEORGICS'

Translated & introduced by
Fred Beake

2024

Published by Arc Publications,
Nanholme Mill, Shaw Wood Road,
Todmorden OL14 6DA, UK
www.arcpublications.co.uk

Translation copyright © Fred Beake, 2024
Introduction copyright © Fred Beake, 2024
Copyright in the present edition © Arc Publications, 2024

978 1911469 88 9

Design by Tony Ward
Printed in the UK by
TJ Books, Padstow, Cornwall

Cover:
Illustration to Virgil's *Georgics*:
'Hiving Bees' by Wenceslaus Hollar, ca. 1654

Acknowledgements

Thanks are due to the editor of *Acumen* where some of these translations first appeared.

This book is in copyright. Subject to statutory exception and to provision of relevant collective licensing agreements, no reproduction of any part of this book may take place without the written permission of Arc Publications.

Arc Chapbook Series
Series Editor: Tony Ward

CONTENTS

Introduction / 4

Book One / 9

Book Two / 15

Book Three / 21

Book Four / 33

Biographical Notes / 44

THE GEORGICS: A BRIEF INTRODUCTION

The four books of the *Georgics* represent Virgil's intermediate poem between the *Eclogues* and the *Aeneid*. The title *Georgicon* means something like 'Country Matters'.

There is no doubt that Virgil (70 BCE to 19 BCE) knew his Greek; Aratus on weather and seasons, say, or Hesiod's *Works and Days* are often in sight; and he definitely had the great Greek Alexandrian poet Callimachus in view as a partial model. Moreover, he undoubtedly made use of his elder contemporary, the Roman author Varo's *Rerum Rusticarum* (On Rural Matters) as a source material. This is all good food for the scholars!

However, having spent over ten years translating the *Georgics*, the scholarly obsession with Virgil's sources does worry me. I tend to see it as a very dreamy poem that picks up on reality when it wants, but goes off by itself when it desires, which, insofar as we know Callimachus (which is not a lot), is very Callimachian.

To understand the *Georgics* and indeed most of Virgil's writing, you must remember that he was born little more than a decade after the long series of internal wars that had wracked the hitherto stable Roman State came to an end with the restoration of the Republic by Sulla in 79 BCE. Indeed, memory of grim civil wars with much proscription and murder of opponents must have been very much part of Virgil's childhood and adolescence. After a thirty year gap, however, civil war resumed with the struggle between Caesar and Pompey. Caesar won, but then, as he seemed about to restore some stability, he was murdered, as lovers of Shakespeare will know. Civil war followed and yet again there was much proscription and often random murder of opponents, that included among its victims the great Cicero. As if that was not enough, the Roman world had then to endure the war between, on the one hand, Mark Antony and his Egyptian ally, Cleopatra, and on the other, Caesar Octavian (the later Emperor Augustus and Julius Caesar's nephew), which only ended at the battle of Actium in 31 BCE, when Virgil was thirty nine

This was just two years before Virgil had the honour of reading the *Georgics* to Caesar Octavian, to whom he had been introduced by the new Roman leader's minister, Maecenas. Therefore (as Richard Thomas[1] points out in his fine commentary) the poem had been worked on at a time in the 30s BCE when there were constant threats to the Roman State and, by implication, to the ordinary Roman. Hence, perhaps, the constant sense of threat and the general uncertainty about Nature in the *Georgics*. Yes, it was part of the Octavian / Maecenas programme of the time to restore an awareness of old Roman values, not least to revive the ancient Yeomanry and indeed the old country gods, as part of a move towards stabilisation of the state, even though both old gods and countryfolk were in decline. However, surely this is something that Virgil, and indeed Horace, believed sincerely. The fascism of the twentieth century cast a strange shadow over Virgil and Horace because of their association with Octavian / Augustus: it was widely claimed that they were merely writing propaganda on behalf of an unpleasant regime. However, in the 20s and 30s BCE, this regime was relatively benign and the two poets were supporting a cause that they deeply believed in. It is of course sad that Octavian eventually became Augustus and the first Emperor, and that he, and his successors even more, became so tyrannical, but it cannot have been at all obvious that this was going to happen when the *Georgics* were written.

A brief word about this translation. I did *Georgics* Book Four for A Level back in the 1960s and was deeply fascinated by it. I tried to translate Book Four in the early '70s, but could not find a form that would flow. In the early 2000s I took a Classics degree late in life at Bristol University and was reintroduced to passages in the *Georgics* by Professor Charles

---

[1] Virgil, *Georgics* edited by Richard F. Thomas, Cambridge University Press, 1988.

Martindale. Some years later still, it occurred to me that a lot of my problems came from Virgil's tendency to compose as much in phrases as in sentences. It struck me that, by adopting the three-part free verse form, that William Carlos Williams used in his later work, calling it the 'variable foot', it would be possible to concentrate on the phrases. After a while I realized this did work, but only if I reduced three lines to two. The kind loan of a converted hayloft out in the Devon countryside by Kevin and Donna Cox made possible a number of bursts of concentrated work. Strangely, I stuck for several years on Book Four, which I knew best, but in the end it was finished to my satisfaction.

Rather like Virgil in Book Four, I had the feeling of being on a constant voyage of discovery, which by a strange process seemed to be also something of a dream journey. I kept thinking of French poet Robert Desnos' fine Surrealist long poem of 1930, 'Night of Loveless Nights', that I translated in the early '70s.[2] In short, though there is much of reality subsumed into the *Georgics*, there is also the sense of a very great poet edging his way through the mental morasses of a difficult time and I hope I have been able to convey something of this without wandering from the original sense.

The selection for this little book tends to choose passages that seem likely to appeal to a modern and not necessarily Classically literate audience, but that also suit the chapbook format. In practice this means that much of the mythology and a lot of the references to Octavian and his minister Maecenas have disappeared; short passages are often taken from rather longer ones; and one or two strange and rather beautiful passages that describe Aristaeus' adventures following the loss of his bees, which lead up to the Orpheus and Eurydice section, have had to be left out, though they include to my mind some of Virgil's best writing. However, contrariwise, I seem to have created an almost Imagist text

---

[2] Available in *The Bees of the Horizon*, translated Fred Beake, Etruscan Books, Buckfastleigh, 2005.

that gives something of the Roman landscape, but also something of the inner mind of a generation hoping for peace after long and bitter civil wars yet still fearful that they may return, which I hope may appeal in its own right.

Fred Beake

ex **GEORGICON LIBRO I**

Vere novo, gelidus canis cum montibus humor   43-56
liquitur et Zephyro putris se glaeba resolvit,
depresso incipiat iam tum mihi taurus aratro
ingemere et sulco attritus splendescere vomer.
Illa seges demum votis respondet avari
agricolae, bis quae solem, bis frigora sensit;
illius inmensae ruperunt horrea messes.
At prius ignotum ferro quam scindimus aequor,
ventos et varium caeli praediscere morem
cura sit ac patrios cultusque habitusque locorum
et quid quaeque ferat regio et quid quaeque recuset.
Hic segetes, illic veniunt felicius uvae,
arborei fetus alibi, atque iniussa virescunt
gramina.

*

from **GEORGICS BOOK ONE**

> *Book One is broadly an introduction to country matters, ploughing and seasonal events; and yet it is full both of the uncertainty of the farmer's life in the face of the seasons, and especially towards the end of the book the instability of the Roman state and the endless Civil Wars of the previous century, which hopefully Octavian Caesar and his great minister Maecenas (who are Virgil's patrons) are going to remedy. The book ends with strangely modern passages about the horror of war and a fear that things will go out of control yet again.*

A new Spring; and frozen waters in the snowy mountains
    turn liquid and clods crumble
at the touch of the South Wind. Time then
    for the bull ox to groan away
as it gets its plough to cut deep
    and the share shines with moisture.
A field only yields the best corn,
    as good as its farmer's desires,
that has felt two season's frost and sun.
    That brings harvests
to burst granaries.

But before we start to break with steel
    somewhere that has not been ploughed before
and whose properties we do not know,
    take care to figure out the winds
and the ways of the sky. Take note
    of the age-long lore of the area.
There will be something that always grows
    and something that never takes.
Here corn does better; and there grapes.
    Here young trees spring and grass grows green,
all of their own accord.

*

...ita turbine nigro 320-31
ferret hiems culmumque levem stipulasque volantis.
Saepe etiam inmensum caelo venit agmen aquarum
et foedam glomerant tempestatem imbribus atris
collectae ex alto nubes; ruit arduus aether
et pluvia ingenti sata laeta boumque labores
diluit; inplentur fossae et cava flumina crescunt
cum sonitu fervetque fretis spirantibus aequor.
Ipse pater media nimborum in nocte corusca
fulmina molitur dextra; quo maxuma motu
terra tremit;

*

Vox quoque per lucos volgo exaudita silentis 476-497
ingens et simulacra modis pallentia miris
visa sub obscurum noctis, pecudesque locutae,
infandum! sistunt amnes terraeque dehiscunt
et maestum inlacrimat templis ebur aeraque sudant.
Proluit insano contorquens vertice silvas
fluviorum rex Eridanus camposque per omnis
cum stabulis armenta tulit. Nec tempore eodem
tristibus aut extis fibrae adparere minaces
aut puteis manare cruor cessavit et altae
per noctem resonare lupis ululantibus urbes.
Non alias caelo ceciderunt plura sereno
fulgura nec diri totiens arsere cometae.
ergo inter sese paribus concurrere telis
Romanas acies iterum videre Philippi;

Then a dark wind winter-born
   whirls stalk and stubble about. And often enough a great column
of waters comes marching out of Heaven.
   Cloud armies gathered from on high
swell the bleak gale with dark showers. The height of Heaven
   has rushed at us and flooded away
the lovely crops, all that work of men and beasts.
   Ditches and drains are full; rivers swell
and roar in their beds; and sea grows passionate in its spumy bays.
   The hand of the Father of Gods gleams through the night's dark
clouds as he deals out lightning and thunder.
   And earth trembles at that mighty motion.
The beasts are in flight; and a humbling shame
   has stricken the hearts
of every man in every nation, as Jupiter hurtles down
   the great mountains, tossing blazing bolts.
Swelling of the gale and rain even thicker, so the woods
   and shores resound with moaning.

*

Huge voice echoing out through the silence of sacred groves
   and heard in terror by the multitude!
Cattle speaking actual words. It was all quite horrible.
   And rivers halting in their courses;
And earth bursting open. Temple statues,
   bronze and ivory alike,
weep or sweat in their grief. And Eridanus,
   monarch of rivers, washed away woods,
whirling insanely out of his course, over all the flat land
   took cattle and byre alike.

Threatening signs appear in entrails to the soothsayers;
   blood does not cease to flow from the wells.
through the darkness mighty cities resound with the howl of wolves.
   Never more lightning out of a clear sky,
never more dire flaming of comets. And so Philippi came to see

nec fuit indignum superis, bis sanguine nostro
Emathiam et latos Haemi pinguescere campos.
Scilicet et tempus veniet, cum finibus illis
agricola incurvo terram molitus aratro
exesa inveniet scabra robigine pila
aut gravibus rastris galeas pulsabit inanis
grandiaque effossis mirabitur ossa sepulchris.

*

... tot bella per orbem, 505-514
tam multae scelerum facies; non ullus aratro
dignus honos, squalent abductis arva colonis
et curvae rigidum falces conflantur in ensem.
Hinc movet Euphrates, illinc Germania bellum;
vicinae ruptis inter se legibus urbes
arma ferunt; saevit toto Mars inpius orbe;
ut cum carceribus sese effudere quadrigae,
addunt in spatia et frustra retinacula tendens
fertur equis auriga neque audit currus habenas.

       two Roman battle lines collide
and brother fighting brother with the same weaponry.
       But the gods above saw nothing improper
when the great plains of Haemus and Emathia
       twice grew fat with our blood.
And indeed, in time to come in those places,
       when the farmer is busy with his curved plough
he will come across javelins half consumed
       by mould and rust. Or one
of his heavy hoes will strike an empty helmet.
       Or he will upturn a burial
and be struck by the size of the bones.

                             *

       So many wars throughout the world;
And evil has so many faces; and, as for the plough
       it has no honour: the fields are waste,
the cultivators removed; and the curve of the pruning hooks
       is become straight swords.
There is action on the Euphrates, action in Germany
       as treaties are broken between neighbouring states
and they fight. Unholy Mars wreaks havoc
       throughout the world. It is just like
when the four-horse chariots burst out from the barriers
       and they add lap to lap, and a driver finds
that pulling the reins brings no response
       and he lacks any control.

ex **GEORGICON LIBRO II**

Nigra fere et presso pinguis sub vomere terra   203-211
et cui putre solum, – namque hoc imitamur arando –
optima frumentis; non ullo ex aequore cernes
plura domum tardis decedere plaustra iuvencis;
aut unde iratus silvam devexit arator
et nemora evertit multos ignava per annos
antiquasque domos avium cum stirpibus imis
eruit; illae altum nidis petiere relictis,
at rudis enituit inpulso vomere campus.

*

from **GEORGICS BOOK TWO**

Book Two has much about vines, trees and a solid yeomanry, but also an unease that Justice has departed from the land. It is rather noticeable that yeomen rather than slaves cultivate the land in Georgics Two. *Some yeomen must have still tilled their own smallholdings when Virgil wrote the Georgics in the 30s B.C., but the big estates largely used slave labour and must have done so since the time of the war with Hannibal. The policy of Virgil's patrons, Octavian and Maecenas, seems however to have favoured a large scale return to the sturdy yeomanry of an older Rome, which had provided apart from anything else a source of quality troops. The automatic grants of land to retired soldiers by the various victors in the Civil Wars were almost certainly meant in part to restore the old yeomanry and their supposedly high level of moral conduct, but also served a military and political purpose. Virgil was decidedly unhappy about the displacement of countrymen to make way for retired soldiers as he makes clear in* Eclogues *1 and 9.*

Ground that is black almost
    and seems rich when ploughed
with soil that is friable,
    which is the aim in ploughing,
now that is what you want for corn.
    Those are the only areas
from which you will observe
    quite so many farm carts
drawn homewards by dawdling bullocks.
    But that is the place also
where the over-eager cultivator
    has carried off the timber
and done away with the woods
    that have stood there, unproductive
for so many years. He has laid low
    the ancient nests of birds
and ripped out the deepest roots.
    And the birds take to the sky
forced to abandon their nests
    and lo! their land is a wreck
and bright with the upturning of the plough.

*

vere tument terrae et genitalia semina poscunt. 324-333
Tum pater omnipotens fecundis imbribus Aether
coniugis in gremium laetae descendit et omnis
magnus alit magno commixtus corpore fetus.
Avia tum resonant avibus virgulta canoris
et Venerem certis repetunt armenta diebus;
parturit almus ager Zephyrique tepentibus auris
laxant arva sinus; superat tener omnibus humor;
inque novos soles audent se germina tuto
credere...

*

O fortunatos nimium, sua si bona norint, 458-474
agricolas! quibus ipsa procul discordibus armis
fundit humo facilem victum iustissima tellus.
Si non ingentem foribus domus alta superbis
mane salutantum totis vomit aedibus undam,
nec varios inhiant pulchra testudine postis
inlusasque auro vestes Ephyreiaque aera,
alba neque Assyrio fucatur lana veneno
nec casia liquidi corrumpitur usus olivi:
at secura quies et nescia fallere vita,
dives opum variarum, at latis otia fundis –

… And in Spring
   the land is eager and demands seed
to bring forth life. Then our mighty Sky-Father
   descends with fertilising showers
into the lap of his joyful mate. His whole might
   joins with her mighty frame
to bring forth the new offspring. And then
   copses resound with melody
and bird with bird is mating. And
   at the due time
the herds are ready for love. The gravid fields
   are ready to produce
and the ploughlands loosen their breasts
   at the feel of soft breezes
from the south. A gentle moisture
   abounds in all things and grasses
dare trust their safety to new suns.

*

Oh they are so fortunate, these ordinary countrymen,
   or would be, if they knew it.
For them the great justice of the earth
   pours forth adequate sustenance
out of the soil, far from the noise of battle.
   What if no great town house
pours out each morning from its antechambers
   a great wave of clients
come to pay their respects and now leaving
   by the proud portals! They may not gape
at doors made beautiful with tortoise shell,
   or clothes inlaid with gold, or the bronzes of Corinth.
They wear white wool no Assyrian dye has poisoned,
   and olive oil goes uncorrupted with cassia.
They possess unsullied quiet
   and a life unaware of lies.
And they are rich in so many ways.
   They can relax in open places

speluncae vivique lacus et frigida Tempe
mugitusque boum
mollesque sub arbore somni –
non absunt; illic saltus ac lustra ferarum
et patiens operum exiguoque adsueta iuventus,
sacra deum sanctique patres; extrema per illos
iustitia excedens terris vestigia fecit.

*

Me vero primum dulces ante omnia Musae, 475-478
quarum sacra fero ingenti percussus amore,
accipiant caelique vias et sidera monstrent,
defectus solis varios lunaeque labores…

by caves and lakes that seem alive; and there are cool vales
    with mooing of cattle and pleasant snoozing
under trees. They miss out on none of these.
    And then there are the glens with their lurking beasts.
And the young men are so steady at their work
    and used to moderation
and practise reverence for gods
    and respect for their fathers. When
the Goddess of Justice upped and left the earth
    it was among these people
that she left her final traces.

*

But as for myself the delicious Muses
    come before anything else.
I am stricken with a great love
    and bear their symbols.
Let them take me and show me
    the pathways of the sky and stars,
the sun's numerous shifts
    and the labours of the moon.

ex GEORGICON LIBRO III

Seu quis Olympiacae miratus praemia palmae 49-91
pascit equos seu quis fortis ad aratra iuvencos,
corpora praecipue matrum legat. Optuma torvae
forma bovis, cui turpe caput, cui plurima cervix,
et crurum tenus a mento palearia pendent;
tum longo nullus lateri modus; omnia magna,
pes etiam; et camuris hirtae sub cornibus aures.
Nec mihi displiceat maculis insignis et albo,
aut iuga detractans interdumque aspera cornu
et faciem tauro propior, quaeque ardua tota,
et gradiens ima verrit vestigia cauda,
Aetas Lucinam iustosque pati hymenaeos
desinit ante decem, post quattuor incipit annos;
cetera nec feturae habilis nec fortis aratris.
Interea, superat gregibus dum laeta iuventas,
solve mares; mitte in Venerem pecuaria primus,

from GEORGICS BOOK THREE

In Book Three we are mainly in the world of beasts, with memorable passages about cattle, horses (which Virgil trained and bred, not least for Octavian) and sheep. However, the book ends with a grimly tragic passage about a plague.

But whether you nourish your horses
  in hopes of Olympian triumphs,
or bullocks to heave the plough mightily,
  pay especial attention to the mother.
The best cow has something of fierceness
  and there is nothing pretty
About her head. She has plenty of neck,
  her dewlaps hang from throat to knee
and her flanks cannot be too long.
  Everything should be on the big side
even her feet; and under twisting horns
  there should be shaggy ears.
And there's nothing to worry about
  if she has odd spots
and white ones at that, or throws off
  the yoke, or gets frisky with her horns.

And if her face resembles a bull's
  it is not a problem. Let her
stand tall and swish her footprints
  with her long tail's tip as she walks.
The right age to bear calves
  and therefore for mating
ceases before the tenth year
  and begins when the cow is four.
For the rest they are no good to breed
  and too weak for ploughing.

Anyhow, when the flocks are full of exuberance
  loose the bulls! Be first
to expose your cattle to Venus' will
  and by breeding each with each
ensure your herd's continuance.

atque aliam ex alia generando suffice prolem.
Optuma quaeque dies miseris mortalibus aevi
prima fugit; subeunt morbi tristisque senectus
et labor, et durae rapit inclementia mortis.
Semper erunt, quarum mutari corpora malis:
semper enim refice ac, ne post amissa requiras,
ante veni et subolem armento sortire quotannis.
Nec non et pecori est idem dilectus equino.
Tu modo, quos in spem statues submittere gentis,
praecipuum iam inde a teneris impende laborem.
Continuo pecoris generosi pullus in arvis
altius ingreditur et mollia crura reponit;
primus et ire viam et fluvios temptare minaces
audet et ignoto sese committere ponti
nec vanos horret strepitus. Illi ardua cervix
argutumque caput, brevis alvus obesaque terga,
luxuriatque toris animosum pectus. Honesti
spadices glaucique, color deterrimus albis

    The best time in this life
is first to pass, for that is the sad lot

    of all creatures. Illness creeps in
with sad old age and endless burdens
    till death that shows no mercy
takes their all. And there will always
    be cattle whose failings
you prefer to breed out. That you should
    continue with; and in case
you should think of it when the chance is lost
    get ahead of yourself and each year
sort out new stock for the herd.

And for that matter whatever is right for cattle,
    it is the same for horses.

To those you intend to raise up
    as the future hope of their kind
from their earliest days
    devote all your energies.

From the very beginning a foal born
    of the best blood steps
about the meadows lifting his legs higher
    than the rest and puts them down

so softly. First to go on adventures
    he dares wild rivers and trusts
the untested bridge; and sounds
    with nothing to them
never frighten him. High neck,
    graceful head, slight belly,
plump back, his spirited breast
    delights in twists of muscle.
The skin of a good horse, now that's
    chestnut or grey, but be put off
by dun or white. And then, if the noise

et gilvo. Tum, si qua sonum procul arma dedere
stare loco nescit, micat auribus et tremit artus
collectumque premens volvit sub naribus ignem.
Densa iuba, et dextro iactata recumbit in armo;
at duplex agitur per lumbos spina, cavatque
tellurem et solido graviter sonat ungula cornu.
Talis Amyclaei domitus Pollucis habenis
Cyllarus et, quorum Grai meminere poetae,
Martis equi biiuges et magni currus Achilli.

*

...patitur meminisse nec herbae   216-221
dulcibus illa quidem inlecebris, et saepe superbos
cornibus inter se subigit decernere amantis.
Pascitur in magna Sila formosa iuvenca:
illi alternantes multa vi proelia miscent
volneribus crebris, lavit ater corpora sanguis...

*

...Nec singula morbi   471-477
corpora corripiunt, sed tota aestiva repente,
spemque gregemque simul cunctamque ab origine gentem.

of battle is near, he has no idea
of staying put, but his ears prick up
   and his limbs shiver. He snorts
and revolves the gathered passion
   in his nostrils. The mane is dense
and he tosses it right over
   his right shoulder. There's
a double line of bone by his loins.
   His solid horn hoof hollows earth
and resonates. Such was Cyllarus
   who that Amyclaean, Pollux,
tamed and harnessed. And then there are
   the horses of the God of War,
great Achilles' chariot pair, that Homer recalls.

*

Her blandishments make him oblivious
   to woods and grass and she frequently
provokes her haughty suitors
   to decide the matter with their horns.
She goes on munching grass
   in Sila's mighty forest,
but the bulls engage in War's
   shifting fortunes with all
Of their strength. There are endless wounds
   and dark blood washes over their bodies.

*

The disease does not just take hold
   of a single body, but all the summer's sheep
at one go, the pick of them
   and the generality, the whole clan of them,
root and branch. So one may know
   high up in the Alps
or among the remains of hill forts in Norica

Tum sciat, aerias Alpis et Norica si quis
castella in tumulis et Iapydis arva Timavi
nunc quoque post tanto videat desertaque regna
pastorum...

*

Hic quondam morbo caeli miseranda coorta est 478-482
tempestas totoque autumni incanduit aestu
et genus omne neci pecudum dedit, omne ferarum,
corrupitque lacus, infecit pabula tabo.
Nec via mortis erat simplex...

*

Saepe in honore deum medio stans hostia ad aram 486-496
lanea dum nivea circumdatur infula vitta,
inter cunctantis cecidit moribunda ministros.
Aut si quam ferro mactaverat ante sacerdos
inde neque impositis ardent altaria fibris
nec responsa potest consultus reddere vates,
ac vix suppositi tinguntur sanguine cultri
summaque ieiuna sanie infuscatur harena.
Hinc laetis vituli volgo moriuntur in herbis
et dulcis animas plena ad praesepia reddunt;
hinc canibus blandis rabies venit et quatit aegros...

*

    or among the fields of the Iapydi
or by the banks of the Timavus, even after so long,
these are the abandoned realms of the shepherd kings.

These empty glades that spread so far
    Were once all theirs.

*

Once the very heaven was sick
    and the grimmest of seasons came from it.
That autumn blazed white with a totally consuming heat
    and handed over to death
farm animal and wild beast. It infected
    lake and pond and pasture.
There was no single road to death.

*

    Often in honour of the gods
the victim was standing in the midst by the altar;
    the snow white band of wool was round its brow;
But the beast dropped dead and the priests
    could not use it for sacrifice. Or, if someone
got busy with his knife and killed the creature earlier on
    then the altars did not glow
when the entrails were laid out on them;
    and the prophet, when asked the question,
had nothing to go on. The sacrificial knives
    are barely tinged with blood
while the surface of the sand
    is scarcely darkened.
And groups of calves are dying among good grass
    and gentle spirits pass
despite plentiful fodder in the byres.

*

Labitur infelix studiorum atque immemor herbae 498-508
victor equus fontisque avertitur et pede terram
crebra ferit; demissae aures, incertus ibidem
sudor et ille quidem morituris frigidus, aret
pellis et ad tactum tractanti dura resistit.
Haec ante exitium primis dant signa diebus;
sin in processu coepit crudescere morbus,
tum vero ardentes oculi atque attractus ab alto
spiritus, interdum gemitu gravis, imaque longo
ilia singultu tendunt, it naribus ater
sanguis...

*

Ecce autem duro fumans sub vomere taurus 515-519
concidit et mixtum spumis vomit ore cruorem
extremosque ciet gemitus. It tristis arator
maerentem abiungens fraterna morte iuvencum,
atque opere in medio defixa relinquit aratra.

*

The victor of so many races
    forgets about grass and gallops,
turns away from water and constantly
    thumps the ground with his hoof.

Ears drooping, his sweat is fitful and cold:
    his death is on its way,
Skin is dry, hard to the stroking hand.

Such are the signs on offer
    in the days before the final passing.
But in the remaining time
    the illness gets more unpleasant.
Eyes blaze and breath is drawn
    from somewhere deep down.

There is fearsome groaning from time to time.
    His flanks shudder with his death sighs
all the way down his body's length;
    And black blood pours from his nostrils.

*

And look at the ox, flanks smoking
    from pulling the plough. Suddenly
he falls down and his mouth is vomiting
    blood and foam and he is uttering
his final groans. The ploughman
    is so full of sadness as he unyokes
the other steer as it grieves for its mate,
    and with the job half done
unfastens the plough.

*

...Atqui non Massica Bacchi 526-530
munera, non illis epulae nocuere repostae:
frondibus et victu pascuntur simplicis herbae,
pocula sunt fontes liquidi atque exercita cursu
flumina, nec somnos abrumpit cura salubris.

*

Iam maris immensi prolem et genus omne natantum 541-543
litore in extremo, ceu naufraga corpora, fluctus
proluit...

*

Ipsis est aër avibus non aequus, et illae 546-548
praecipites alta vitam sub nube relinquunt,
praeterea iam nec pabula refert...

*

Saevit et in lucem Stygiis emissa tenebris 551-557
pallida Tisiphone Morbos agit ante Metumque,
inque dies avidum surgens caput altius effert:
Balatu pecorum et crebris mugitibus amnes
arentesque sonant ripae collesque supini:
Iamque catervatim dat stragem atque aggerat ipsis
in stabulis...

*

    It is not as if he was ruined
by heady wine from Mount Massicus
    in the course of repeated feasting.
No, the way of him and his kind
    is to feed on simple grass and leaves.
Instead of wine cups they have clear springs
    and rivers that race along;
and their sleep is healthy and unbroken by worries.

*

    And now
    the progeny of the great ocean,
all creatures that swim are washed onto the shore
    by the waves and look like shipwrecked men.

*

Air becomes useless for the birds and they die
    tumbling headlong from beneath the clouds.
and no change of diet has any effect; even
    the remedies do harm.

*

Pallid Tisiphone is making mayhem. She has been dispatched
    into the light out of the shadowy banks of Styx.
She drives disease and fear before her
    and every day lifts higher her greedy head.
With bleating of sheep and ceaseless mooing
    the dried up brooks and hill slopes echo.
And now she gives them all to slaughter
    heaping the bodies in the folds
as they fall apart with the plague.

*

ex **GEORGICON LIBRO IV**

Protinus aerii mellis caelestia dona 1-7
exsequar: hanc etiam, Maecenas, adspice partem.
Admiranda tibi levium spectacula rerum
magnanimosque duces totiusque ordine gentis
5mores et studia et populos et proelia dicam.
In tenui labor; at tenuis non gloria, si quem
numina laeva sinunt auditque vocatus Apollo.

*

from **GEORGICS BOOK FOUR**

Book Four is in many ways the odd one out. Ostensibly it is about bees, who are treated in a very playful fashion as a mirror of human civilisation, but the second half is devoted to the very strange, yet compelling story of the shepherd Aristaeus. He has lost his bees and must go through strange adventures to reclaim them; these have had to be left out for reasons of space. However, this strange fantasy leads to one of the great passages of ancient literature, the story of Orpheus and Eurydice, which ends these selections from the Georgics. *The much later Roman commentator Servius believed this rather strange conclusion to* Georgics Book Four *was inserted because it originally ended with an elaborate praise song for Gallus, a poet and friend of Virgil, but also Imperial administrator, who was executed by Octavian for treason. However* Eclogue 10 *is very much addressed to Gallus and that was not altered. It seems more likely that Virgil was following Callimachus' practice of odd insertions into longer poems. Catullus' sixty-fourth poem of about two decades earlier, which Virgil almost certainly knew, also borrows the Callimachian device of inserting a story within a story. Possibly our poet was just a little bored with his bees! On several occasions in this book Virgil says he is tired of his long voyage (i.e. his progress through his poem). I am always tempted, rightly or wrongly, to see in Book Four something perhaps of the origins of those strange ethereal creatures in the* Rape of the Lock, *but also perhaps the fine Bee poems of Sylvia Plath.*

Next, of honey, which is a thing of the air
    and a gift of Heaven. Now, Maecenas,
do not get bored with this part of my poem.
    You will find much to interest you
in these miniature states. Their nobles are
    not that different to ours and I am going
to inform you about their tendencies and customs,
    clans, and wars. A slight subject,
but the glory is not slight, if the dubious powers
    of the left permit and Apollo hears when called.

*

Principio sedes apibus statioque petenda, 8-20
quo neque sit ventis aditus nam pabula venti
ferre domum prohibent neque oves haedique petulci
floribus insultent aut errans bucula campo
decutiat rorem et surgentes atterat herbas.
Absint et picti squalentia terga lacerti
pinguibus a stabulis meropesque aliaeque volucres
et manibus Procne pectus signata cruentis;
omnia nam late vastant ipsasque volantes
ore ferunt dulcem nidis immitibus escam.
At liquidi fontes et stagna virentia musco
adsint et tenuis fugiens per gramina rivus,
palmaque vestibulum aut ingens oleaster inumbret...

*

Atque equidem, extremo ni iam sub fine laborum 116-124
vela traham et terris festinem advertere proram,
forsitan et, pingues hortos quae cura colendi
ornaret, canerem, biferique rosaria Paesti,
quoque modo potis gauderent intiba rivis
et virides apio ripae, tortusque per herbam
cresceret in ventrem cucumis; nec sera comantem
narcissum aut flexi tacuissem vimen acanthi
pallentesque hederas et amantes litora myrtos.

*

First, you need a dwelling for the bees,
    a definite place must be found:
no way in for winds, to stop
    the bee carrying supplies back home
and on no account let a mother sheep or butting kid
    mess up the flowers,
or a plain-wandering heifer shake off the dew
    and stop the grass from pushing up straight.
No! You want none of these, and equally
    the coloured one of the scaly back
must have no entrance to these honeyed halls,
    or the birds that eat bees
or he whose breast is marked with the bloody hands of Procne.
    Admit none that saunter about the skies
looking to carry a nice dinner
    back to to their nest and loved ones.
But you do need clear springs and pools green with moss
    and a little creeping stream to meander through the grass;
And the shade of a palm or wild olive over the entrance.

*

But if I were not at the end of all my work,
    about to furl sails
and turn my prow towards the land
    I might well go on
about how carefulness brings ornament
    to flower gardens
and of Paestum and its twice yearly roses.
    Not to mention the endive
happy in its drinkable streams and the banks
    green with celery. And creeping
through the grass the cucumber swelling. The narcissus
    of course flowers late;
and I cannot leave out the twigs
    of the twisting acanthus,
or pale ivy, or the myrtle that loves the stream edge.

*

Namque sub Oebaliae memini me turribus arcis, 128-132
qua niger umectat flaventia culta Galaesus,
Corycium vidisse senem, cui pauca relicti
iugera ruris erant, nec fertilis illa iuvencis
nec pecori opportuna seges nec commoda Baccho.
Hic rarum tamen in dumis olus albaque circum
lilia verbenasque premens vescumque papaver
regum aequabat opes...

*

Ipse cava solans aegrum testudine amorem 464-527
te, dulcis coniunx, te solo in litore secum,
te veniente die, te decedente canebat.
Taenarias etiam fauces, alta ostia Ditis,
et caligantem nigra formidine lucum
ingressus manesque adiit regemque tremendum
nesciaque humanis precibus mansuescere corda.

       But now by Oebalia I remember
beneath the towers of the citadel where the black waters
         of Galaesus water the yellow crops
I have watched an old man, a Cilician. He ruled
         a few acres of abandoned land.
The grass was no use for bullocks or cattle
         and hopeless for vines.
But here and there among the brambles he put in
         some vegetables, but also white lilies
and vervain and some little poppies and his soul
              was on a level with kings.

*

In the full text we now come to the shepherd Aristaeus, who has lost his bees to a plague and believes he is cursed. He makes a visit to his semi-divine mother in caves deep under ground. She tells him how to get the reasons for his cursing out of Proteus, the Old Man of the Sea, which he does successfully. It emerges that Aristaeus was accidentally responsible for the death of Eurydice. This turns into an excuse for Virgil to tell the story of Orpheus' grief at the loss of his true love, of how he redeemed her from the Underworld, of how he lost her a second time, and of his own sad end.

ORPHEUS LOSES EURYDICE

He tried to soothe his love sickness with the hollow lyre
    at the coming of day
and the going down of day. Through Taenarian jaws
    and the tall gates of Dis
and that grey grove that is black with terror
    he went. He approaches
the spirits of the dead and their terrible monarch
    whose hearts have never
 been known to soften in the face
    of human prayer.

At cantu commotae Erebi de sedibus imis
umbrae ibant tenues simulacraque luce carentum,
quam multa in foliis avium se milia condunt
vesper ubi aut hibernus agit de montibus imber,
matres atque viri defunctaque corpora vita
magnanimum heroum, pueri innuptaeque puellae,
impositique rogis iuvenes ante ora parentum,
quos circum limus niger et deformis harundo
Cocyti tardaque palus inamabilis unda
alligat et noviens Styx interfusa coercet.
Quin ipsae stupuere domus atque intima Leti
tartara caeruleosque implexae crinibus angues
Eumenides, tenuitque inhians tria Cerberus ora
atque Ixionii vento rota constitit orbis.
Iamque pedem referens casus evaserat omnes;
redditaque Eurydice superas veniebat ad auras,
pone sequens, namque hanc dederat Proserpina legem,
cum subita incautum dementia cepit amantem,
ignoscenda quidem, scirent si ignoscere manes.

Yet stirred by his chanting
   from the deepest realms of Erebus
came slight shadows and images lacking
   any reality. They were like
the many thousands of birds that hide themselves
   among the leaves while evening
or winter stirs a shower out of the mountains.
   Mothers and husbands
and the heroes of great soul whose bodily life
   is now done. And boys and girls
that did not get to marry. And young men
   placed on the funeral pyre
before their father's eyes. And round about them
   the black slime and misshaped reeds
of Cocytus and its unkindly marsh
   with its slow moving waves
binds them in. And ninefold Styx pouring round
   ensures that they remain.
But they were bewildered, even the inhabitants
   of the house of death
and the depths of Tartarus; and the Furies
   with the dark blue snakes
caught up in their hair. Cerberus stood there, threefold mouth gaping.
   And Ixion's wheel halted with the wind.

Now his feet had avoided every accident.
   Eurydice had been returned.
She was coming where you can feel
   the breezes of the sky above you.
She followed behind, for Proserpine
   had laid down that command.
Suddenly madness took her incautious lover.
   It would have been forgiven,
if the Dead knew how to forgive. He stopped.

Restitit Eurydicenque suam iam luce sub ipsa
immemor heu! victusque animi respexit. Ibi omnis
effusus labor atque immitis rupta tyranni
foedera, terque fragor stagnis auditus Avernis.

Illa, Quis et me, inquit, miseram et te perdidit, Orpheu,
quis tantus furor? En iterum crudelia retro
Fata vocant, conditque natantia lumina somnus.
Iamque vale: feror ingenti circumdata nocte
invalidasque tibi tendens, heu non tua, palmas!â€
dixit et ex oculis subito, ceu fumus in auras
commixtus tenues, fugit diversa, neque illum,
prensantem nequiquam umbras et multa volentem
dicere, praeterea vidit, nec portitor Orci
amplius obiectam passus transire paludem.
Quid faceret? Quo se rapta bis coniuge ferret?
Quo fletu Manis, quae numina voce moveret?
Illa quidem Stygia nabat iam frigida cumba.
Septem illum totos perhibent ex ordine menses
rupe sub aeria deserti ad Strymonis undam

      He looked back
at his dear Eurydice as they came into
    the light of the Earth; he had lost
control of his mind. The result of his great labour
    flowed away as the agreement
with the unremitting tyrant was broken.
    Threefold thunder
was heard among the marshes of Avernus.
    She cried out
'Orpheus, what is it? What has condemned me
    to eternal misery – and you – ?
What enormous madness is it? But
    the Fates call me back
with all their dreadful cruelty once again;
    and sleep shuts up eyes
that are awash with tears. I am carried off.
    Huge darkness
is all around me. I stretch out towards yours
    my hands that have lost their force.
Alas! They will never be yours.' So she said
    and abruptly went from his eyes
like a flicker of smoke on the breeze
    in the other direction.
He clutches uselessly at the shadows,
    there was so much he wanted to say,
but she does not see. And the Ferryman
    of Orcus did not allow him
to pass through the obstacle of the marsh again.
    What was he to do?
His wife had been snatched away twice.
    Where should he go?
What tears, what words, would move
    the other realm of the Dead?
Now she was cold and floating
    in the Stygian barge.
Seven months in all, the legend says,
    Orpheus wept.
At the foot of a sky-reaching crag
    by the lonely waters of Strymon

flesse sibi et gelidis haec evolvisse sub antris
mulcentem tigres et agentem carmine quercus;
qualis populea maerens philomela sub umbra
amissos queritur fetus, quos durus arator
observans nido implumes detraxit; at illa
flet noctem ramoque sedens miserabile carmen
integrat et maestis late loca questibus implet.
Nulla Venus, non ulli animum flexere hymenaei.
Solus Hyperboreas glacies Tanaimque nivalem
arvaque Rhipaeis numquam viduata pruinis
lustrabat raptam Eurydicen atque inrita Ditis
dona querens; spretae Ciconum quo munere matres
inter sacra deum nocturnique orgia Bacchi
discerptum latos iuvenem sparsere per agros.
Tum quoque marmorea caput a cervice revulsum
gurgite cum medio portans Oeagrius Hebrus
volveret, Eurydicen vox ipsa et frigida lingua
ah miseram Eurydicen! anima fugiente vocabat:
Eurydicen toto referebant flumine ripae.

*

in an icy cave he poured forth his feelings.
    He soothed the tiger
and stirred the oak by his song.
    It was just as when under a shady poplar tree
a nightingale grieves for her lost young.
    A coarse ploughman
noticed them and plucked them from the nest
    before they grew feathers;
And she weeps in the darkness and from that branch
    fills the world
with the grief of her song. In the same way
    there was no diverting his spirit;
there were no love songs and no wedding hymns.
    But then by himself, by icy Hyperborean realms
and where the frosty Tanais flows
    and Ryphaean meadows never lose their frost
he went to cleanse his sin. And as he went
    he mourned for Eurydice snatched from him
and Pluto's gift taken back again. But
    some South Thracian mothers
despised him for that very gift. They were
    in the midst of sacred rituals
and nocturnal Bacchic orgies and they ripped
    that young man to pieces
and scattered him through the fields.
    Then his head, torn from its marble-white neck
was being rolled in mid stream. Hebrus
    his own father's river bore it;
and though voice and tongue were numb
    even as the spirit departed
the head cried out, 'Oh my poor Eurydice!'
    And 'Eurydice!'
the river banks re-echoed all the way along.'

*

BIOGRAPHICAL NOTES

PUBLIUS VERGILIUS MARO, or Virgil to us, was born near Mantua in 70 BCE. He was the son of a locally important family, who had him well educated at Cremona and Milan and eventually at Rome. This was probably with an eye to a career in the law courts and politics. However, he chose to return home and work on his poetry at a time when literature was not a normal career for a Roman gentleman. Possibly the civil war between Pompey and Caesar played a part in his decision to come home, but at all events, he began the very slow deliberate composition of his major poems.

First came the *Eclogues*, with their ideal country scenes between shepherds, though they also reflect local families' being deprived of their farms to provide holdings for the veterans of the winning side in the civil wars. The *Eclogues* seem to have caught the attention of Octavian's minister Maecenas, who became Virgil's patron.

Virgil worked on the *Georgics* in the 30s BCE, but also appears to have gained a reputation for training racehorses. Maecenas introduced him to Octavian, who seems to have been greatly taken with this new and radical poetry.

After completing the *Georgics*, Virgil worked on the *Aeneid* until his death in 19 BCE. This was an attempt to tell the mythical story of the Trojan ancestors of the Romans after the sack of Troy and their emigration to Italy, and provides Rome with an epic on the scale of the *Odyssey* and *Iliad*. Though this great poem was very slightly unfinished, and the dying Virgil wanted it to be destroyed, Octavian (now formally elevated to head of the Roman State as Augustus) insisted on its publication after the poet's death.

FRED BEAKE was born in 1948 in Cheshire. He grew up in remote countryside there and in the West Riding. His early education was at East Keswick Primary School and Tadcaster Grammar. He went rather abortively to Sussex University when young, and holds a Classics degree from Bristol, where he went in middle age. He has devoted a lot of his life to poetry, when not being a hands-on father and working as a gardener, van driver, or at other jobs.

He has translated widely from modern French, especially Desnos, Char and Deguy, classical Latin and, more recently, classical Greek, notably Aristophanes' *Peace* for the University of Pennsylvania Press. He edited Mammon Press and *The Poet's Voice* magazine in the eighties and nineties. He published a number of pamphlets of his own poetry in the 1970s and 1980s (notably *The Fisher Queen*, Northern House, 1988), which were collected in *The Whiteness of Her Becoming* (Salzburg UP, 1992).

Since then he has published six volumes of poetry, notably *The Cyclops* (Menard Press, 2002), *New and Selected Poems* (Shearsman, 2006), and the *Old Outlaw* (Shoestring, 2011). His most recent collection is *Out of Silence* (Poetry Salzburg). He has reviewed for *Acumen*, *Stand* and other magazines.

Since 2003 he has been living in Torquay, Devon. He has two children and four granchildren.